G000297280

The Songs of Rodgers & Hammerstein

19 Songs from 8 Musicals

Oklahoma!
THE SOUND OF MUSIC
Me and Juliet
The King and I
CAROUSEL
STATE FAIR
FLOWER DRUM SONG
Cinderella

Interior photos provided courtesy of The Rodgers & Hammerstein Organization

ISBN 978-1-4234-7474-6

WILLIAMSON MUSIC®

A RODGERS AND HAMMERSTEIN COMPANY

www.williamsonmusic.com

EXCLUSIVELY DISTRIBUTED BY

HAL•LEONARD®
CORPORATION

7777 W. BLUEMOUND RD. P.O. BOX 13819 MILWAUKEE, WI 53213

Visit Hal Leonard Online at
www.HalLeonard.com

Richard Rodgers (left) and Oscar Hammerstein II

TABLE OF CONTENTS

PERFORMERS ON THE RECORDINGS

Beverly O'Regan Thiele . . . . Performance Tracks 1-2, 4, 6-12, 13, 17-19

Martha Cares. . . . . Performance Tracks 3, 13-15

Jenna Looker . . . . Performance Track 5

Richard Walters, pianist for all tracks except performance and accompaniment tracks 3, played by John Reed, accompaniment track 5, played by Christopher Ruck, and performance and accompaniment tracks 14-15, played by Sue Malmberg.

RODGERS & HAMMERSTEIN

After long and highly distinguished careers with other collaborators, Richard Rodgers (composer) and Oscar Hammerstein II (librettist/lyricist) joined forces to create the most consistently fruitful and successful partnership in the American musical theatre.

Prior to his work with Hammerstein, Richard Rodgers (1902-1979) collaborated with lyricist Lorenz Hart on a series of musical comedies that epitomized the wit and sophistication of Broadway in its heyday. Prolific on Broadway, in London and in Hollywood from the '20s into the early '40s, Rodgers & Hart wrote more than 40 shows and film scores. Among their greatest were ON YOUR TOES, BABES IN ARMS, THE BOYS FROM SYRACUSE, I MARRIED AN ANGEL and PAL JOEY.

Throughout the same era Oscar Hammerstein II (1895-1960) brought new life to a moribund art form: the operetta. His collaborations with such preeminent composers as Rudolf Friml, Sigmund Romberg and Vincent Youmans resulted in such operetta classics as THE DESERT SONG, ROSE-MARIE, and THE NEW MOON. With Jerome Kern he wrote SHOW BOAT, the 1927 operetta that changed the course of modern musical theatre. His last musical before embarking on an exclusive partnership with Richard Rodgers was CARMEN JONES, the highly-acclaimed 1943 all-black revision of Georges Bizet's tragic opera CARMEN.

OKLAHOMA!, the first Rodgers & Hammerstein musical, was also the first of a new genre, the musical play, representing a unique fusion of Rodgers' musical comedy and Hammerstein's operetta. A milestone in the development of the American musical, it also marked the beginning of the most successful partnership in Broadway musical history, and was followed by CAROUSEL, ALLEGRO, SOUTH PACIFIC, THE KING AND I, ME AND JULIET, PIPE DREAM, FLOWER DRUM SONG and THE SOUND OF MUSIC. Rodgers & Hammerstein wrote one musical specifically for the big screen, STATE FAIR, and one for television, CINDERELLA. Collectively, the Rodgers & Hammerstein musicals earned 35 Tony Awards, 15 Academy Awards, two Pulitzer Prizes, two Grammy Awards and 2 Emmy Awards. In 1998 Rodgers & Hammerstein were cited by Time Magazine and CBS News as among the 20 most influential artists of the 20th century and in 1999 they were jointly commemorated on a U.S. postage stamp.

Despite Hammerstein's death in 1960, Rodgers continued to write for the Broadway stage. His first solo entry, NO STRINGS, earned him two Tony Awards for music and lyrics, and was followed by DO I HEAR A WALTZ?, TWO BY TWO, REX and I REMEMBER MAMA. Richard Rodgers died on December 30, 1979, less than eight months after his last musical opened on Broadway. In March of 1990, Broadway's 46th Street Theatre was renamed The Richard Rodgers Theatre in his honor.

At the turn of the 21st century, the Rodgers and Hammerstein legacy continues to flourish, as marked by the enthusiasm that greeted their Centennials, in 1995 and 2002 respectively.

In 1995, Hammerstein's centennial was celebrated worldwide with commemorative recordings, books, concerts and an award-winning PBS special, "Some Enchanted Evening." The ultimate tribute came the following season, when he had three musicals playing on Broadway simultaneously: SHOW BOAT (1995 Tony Award winner, Best Musical Revival); THE KING AND I (1996 Tony Award winner, Best Musical Revival); and STATE FAIR (1996 Tony Award nominee for Best Score.)

In 2002, the Richard Rodgers Centennial was celebrated around the world, with tributes from Tokyo to London, from the Hollywood Bowl to the White House, featuring six new television specials, museum retrospectives, a dozen new ballets, half a dozen books, new recordings and countless concert and stage productions (including three simultaneous revivals on Broadway, matching Hammerstein's feat of six years earlier), giving testament to the enduring popularity of Richard Rodgers and the sound of his music.

THE SONGS & SHOWS

Songs are in Original Keys except where noted.

CAROUSEL
Broadway Opening: April 19, 1945
London Opening: June 7, 1950
Broadway Revivals: 1949, 1954, 1957, 1994
London Revival: 2008
Film Release: February 16, 1956

Based on the play Liliom by Ferenc Molnar, *Carousel* is set in a small town on the New England coast, 1873-1888.

"Mister Snow" is sung by Carrie Pipperidge (the second female lead) to Julie Jordan after Julie has met Billy Bigelow, the excitable carousel barker who has just been fired. Carrie tells Julie of her own secret romance with fisherman Enoch Snow.

"If I Loved You" comes from an extended amusement park scene soon after the first meeting of Julie Jordan, a mill worker, and Billy Bigelow. Julie has just told Billy that she has never had a boyfriend and will never marry. But her real romantic feelings, shown in the long musical lines of this song, contradict those declarations. First Julie sings the song. Then, with a different verse, Billy sings it.

Julie and Billy love one another, but have a challenging marriage; Billy abuses her. He seems to be a magnet for trouble, and is far from an attentive husband. In a clambake scene that opens Act II, the other girls lightly complain about their men, but Julie, who understand more than they about suffering through a troubled relationship, soulfully replies with **"What's the Use of Wond'rin'."**

Billy gets mixed up with some thugs and attempts a robbery. Billy is caught by the would-be victim, who vows to hand him over to the police with the prospect of a prison term. Cornered, disgraced and terrified for Julie and their unborn child, Billy stabs himself. He dies in Julie's arms. Nettie Fowler, the maternal figure in the show, sings **"You'll Never Walk Alone"** to give Julie comfort and hope. The song is repeated at the end of the show, years later, at the graduation of Julie and Billy's daughter.

CINDERELLA (television)
First Broadcast (live): March 31, 1957
First Remake for Television, First Broadcast: February 22, 1965
Second Remake for Television, First Broadcast: November 2, 1997

Though never officially on Broadway or in London's West End, stage versions of the musical have been produced since 1961.

Based on the fairy tale, *Cinderella* (source: *Cendrillon, ou la Petite Pantoufle de Vair* by Charles Perrault) was the first original musical written for television. Its original live broadcast in 1957, starring Julie Andrews, drew the largest television audience to date of 107,000,000 people. A new color television version was made in 1965, starring Lesley Ann Warren. The 1997 television film starred Brandy Norwood, with other songs by Rodgers interpolated into the score.

Abused and unappreciated by her stepmother and stepsisters, Cinderella sits by the fireplace alone and sings **"In My Own Little Corner."**

FLOWER DRUM SONG
Broadway Opening: December 1, 1958
London Opening: March 24, 1960
Broadway Revival: 2002
Film Release: November 9, 1961

Based on the novel by C.Y. Lee, *Flower Drum Song* takes place in Chinatown of San Francisco. It highlights the generational differences between the young Chinese-Americans and their more traditional parents.

Helen Chao, a seamstress, is in love with Wang Ta, who is engaged to another woman. She sings of her predicament in **"Love, Look Away."** Presented in the original soprano key here, this song was transposed down to a lower key for the 2002 Broadway revival.

THE KING AND I

Broadway Opening: March 29, 1951
London Opening: October 8, 1953
Broadway Revivals: 1977, 1985, 1996
London Revivals: 1979, 2000
Film Release: June 26, 1956
Animated Film Release: March 19, 1999

Based on the novel *Anna and the King of Siam* by Margaret Langdon, the story takes place in Bangkok, Siam, early 1860s. Anna Leonowens is a young widowed teacher from England brought by the king to educate his many children.

As Anna and her son Louis approach their new home, Louis confesses his anxiety at living in a new and unfamiliar environment. Anna reassures her son and herself by singing **"I Whistle a Happy Tune."**

Tuptim, a young Burmese woman presented to the King of Siam as a gift from the Prince of Burma, arrives escorted by courtier Lun Tha. Tuptim and Lun Tha have fallen in love. The King receives his new wife Tuptim with little ceremony, and leaves her alone to regard her dire circumstances in **"My Lord and Master."**

"Hello, Young Lovers" is sung by Anna Leonowens as she reflects sympathetically on the relationship between Tuptim and Lun Tha.

Anna, beginning to settle into her new life in Siam, connects with the king's children singing **"Getting to Know You."**

Lun Tha and Tuptim have been meeting in secret with Anna as lookout. The threat of the King's wrath prompts them to sing **"We Kiss in a Shadow."**

The lovers Lun Tha and Tuptim have decided to escape the court of Siam, risking great danger, and sing **"I Have Dreamed"** in anticipation of being away together.

ME AND JULIET

Broadway Opening: May 28, 1953

With an original book by Oscar Hammerstein II, *Me and Juliet* is a backstage musical comedy that takes place in and around the theatre where the musical, "Me and Juliet," in a Broadway try-out run is playing. Scenes and songs between the characters in the company are interspersed with scenes and songs from the show within the show.

"No Other Love" is sung by Jeanie, a chorus singer in the show, in love with Larry, an assistant stage manager. The melody was adapted by Richard Rodgers from his score for the television documentary series *Victory at Sea*.

OKLAHOMA!

Broadway Opening: March 31, 1943
London Opening: April 29, 1947
Broadway Revivals: 1951, 1953, 1979, 2002
London Revivals: 1980, 1998
Film Release: October 11, 1955

Oklahoma!, based on the play *Green Grow the Lilacs* by Lynn Riggs, is set in the summer of 1907 just prior to the admission of the Indian territory Oklahoma as a state.

Laurey and her girlfriends are at her Aunt Eller's to rest and spruce up for the upcoming box social. Cowboy Curly and Laurey have had flirtatious semi-courtship. She sees another girl making eyes with Curly, but flippantly declares to her friends in **"Many a New Day"** that she will wait for another man.

Laurey, following a sniff of smelling salts from the mysterious peddler Ali Hakim, enters a trance, portrayed in the show as an extended ballet ("Dream Sequence"). She observes both of the men who are vying for her affections, Curly and Jud. Singing **"Out of My Dreams,"** Laurey unleashes her suppressed desire to have Curly, as she watches in horror the menacing Jud Fry overcome him.

THE SOUND OF MUSIC
Broadway Opening: November 16, 1959
London Opening: May 18, 1961
Broadway Revival: 1998
London Revivals: 1981, 2006
Film Release: March, 2, 1965

Set in Austria in 1938 before and during the Anschluss (The Nazi annexing of Austria to Germany), *The Sound of Music* is based on the book *The Trapp Family Singers* by Maria Augusta Trapp. Maria, a young woman intending to become a nun, joins the household of widower Captain von Trapp as governess to his seven children. Maria brings music back into the house. She and the Captain unexpectedly fall in love, ending the Captain's engagement to the Baroness. After Maria and the Captain marry, they escape Austria and the Nazis.

As the show opens, Maria Rainer sings **"The Sound of Music"** admiring the Alps outside of the Abbey where she lives. She gives evidence of her free spirit, appreciation of nature, and her love of song before she is reminded of her duties that she has been neglecting.

In the film version, **"My Favorite Things"** is sung by Maria to the von Trapp children to distract them during a particularly frightening thunderstorm. In the original stage version, the song occurs much earlier. The Mother Abbess, while chastising Maria for her inattentiveness, asks Maria about a song she has heard the apologetic novice singing. They sing **"My Favorite Things"** together.

Maria, afraid of the new feelings she has for Captain von Trapp, returns to the Abby. The wise Mother Abbess offers Maria encouragement in deciding to face Captain von Trapp, singing **"Climb Ev'ry Mountain."**

Maria's songs were originally in a lower key for the stage musical, transposed up to a soprano range for the film. The movie keys are used in this volume.

STATE FAIR (film)
Film Release: August 20, 1945
Film Remake Release: March 15, 1962
Stage Version, Broadway Opening: March 27, 1996

Based on Phil Strong's novel by the same title, *State Fair* takes place in Iowa, 1946. This is Rodgers and Hammerstein's only original film score. The film was released in 1945, and remade in 1962 with a change in the setting to Texas. A stage adaptation opened on Broadway in 1996.

It is August. Farm girl Margy Frake prepares to attend the Iowa Sate Fair with her family. Feeling unsettled and expectant of something to come, she sings **"It Might as Well Be Spring."** The song has been transposed up into a comfortable soprano key for this volume.

IF I LOVED YOU

from *Carousel*

Lyrics by Oscar Hammerstein II
Music by Richard Rodgers

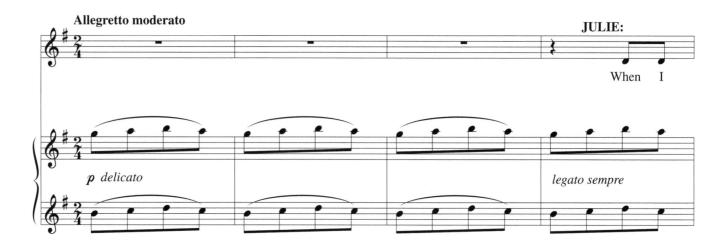

JULIE:

When I

worked in the mill Weav-in' at the loom, I'd gaze ab-sent-

mind-ed at the roof._____ And half the time the shut-tle 'd

WHAT'S THE USE OF WOND'RIN'

from *Carousel*

Music by Richard Rodgers
Lyrics by Oscar Hammerstein II

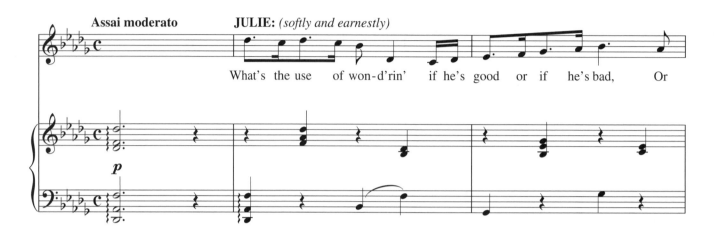

What's the use of won-d'rin' if he's good or if he's bad, Or

if you like the way he wears his hat? Oh! what's the use of won-d'rin', If he's

good or if he's bad? He's your fel - ler and you love him. That's all there is to

There's noth - in' more to say.

Some - thin' made him the way that he is, ___ Wheth - er he's false ___ or

true And some - thin' gave him the things that are his ___

One of those things ___ is you. So When he wants your kiss - es you will

MISTER SNOW

from *Carousel*

Lyrics by Oscar Hammerstein II
Music by Richard Rodgers

Moderato con grazia
CARRIE:

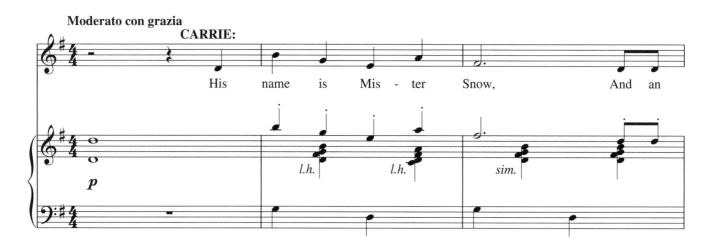

His name is Mis - ter Snow, And an

up - stand - in' man is he. He comes home ev - 'ry night in his

round - bot - tomed boat With a net full of her - ring from the sea.

An al-most per-fect beau, As re-fined as a girl could

wish, But he spends so much time in his round-bot-tomed boat, That he

can't seem to lose the smell of fish! The

fust time he kissed me, the whiff of his clo'es Knocked me flat on the floor of the

deed, Miss Pipp - er - idge, if you'll be mine, I'll be yours fer the rest of my

life!" Next mo - ment we were prom - ised! And

now my mind's in a maze, Fer all it ken do is look

for - ward to That won - der - ful day of days.

Refrain

Moderato *(with expression)*

When I mar - ry Mis - ter Snow,

p dolce

The flow - ers 'll be buz - zin' with the hum of bees, The

mf

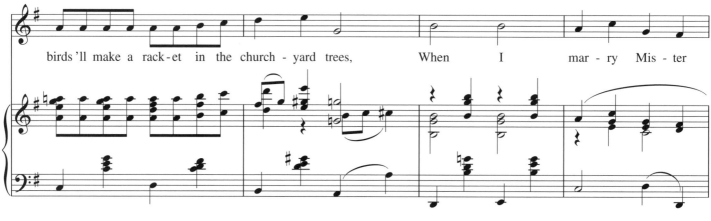

birds 'll make a rack - et in the church - yard trees, When I mar - ry Mis - ter

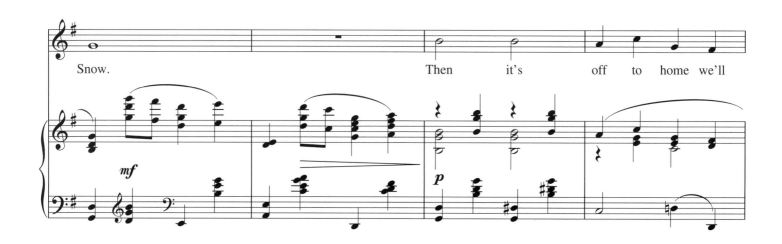

Snow. Then it's off to home we'll

mf

p

YOU'LL NEVER WALK ALONE
from *Carousel*

Lyrics by Oscar Hammerstein II
Music by Richard Rodgers

IN MY OWN LITTLE CORNER

from *Cinderella*

Lyrics by Oscar Hammerstein II
Music by Richard Rodgers

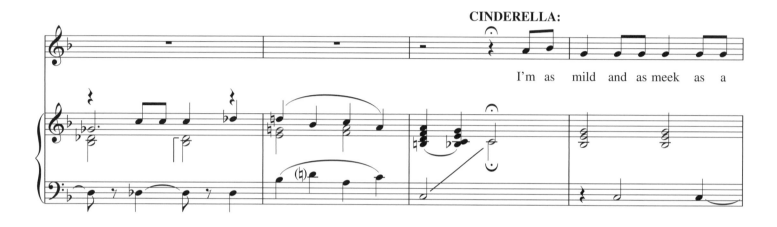

CINDERELLA:

I'm as mild and as meek as a

mouse, When I hear a com-mand I o-bey. But I know of a spot in my

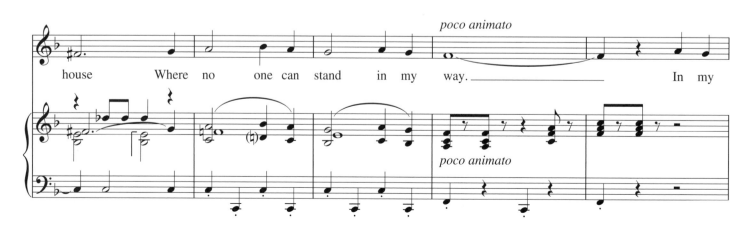

house Where no one can stand in my way. In my

own lit - tle cor - ner, in my own lit - tle chair, I can

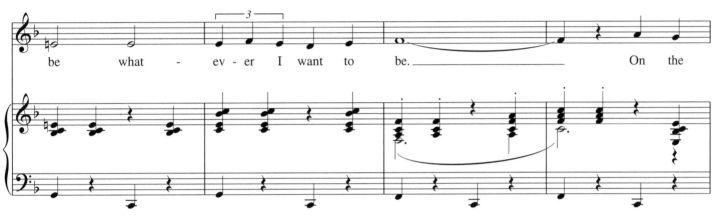

be what - ev - er I want to be. _____ On the

wing of my fan - cy I can fly an - y - where And the

world will o - pen its arms to me. _____ I'm a

young Nor - we - gian prin - cess or a milk maid, _____ I'm the

great - est pri - ma don - na in Mi - lan, _____ I'm an

heir - ess who has al - ways had her silk made _____ By her

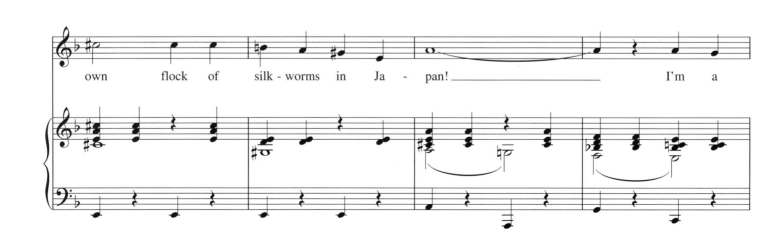

own flock of silk - worms in Ja - pan! _____ I'm a

hunt - ress on an Af - ri - can sa - fa - ri _____ (It's a

dang - 'rous type of sport and yet it's fun); _____ In the

night I sal - ly forth to seek my quar - ry, _____ And I

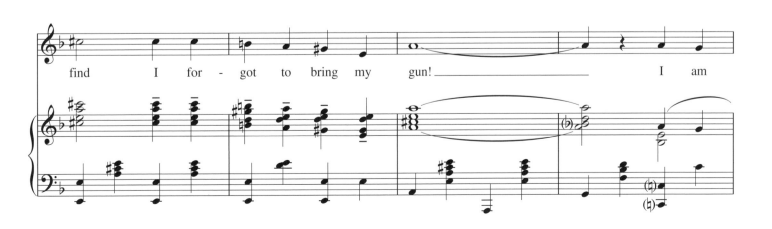

find I for - got to bring my gun! _____ I am

LOVE, LOOK AWAY

from *Flower Drum Song*

Lyrics by Oscar Hammerstein II
Music by Richard Rodgers

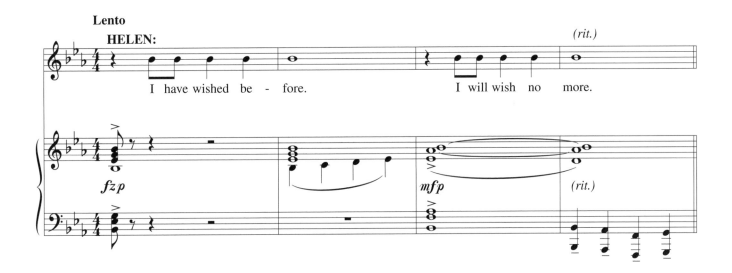

Love, look a - way,_____ Lone - ly though I may be,

Leave me and set me free,_____ Look a - way, look a - way, look a -

poco rit.

mf

poco rit. e più espr.

way from me. me._____

opt.

1.

2.

f

The optional notes, for the final time, are editorial suggestions.

I WHISTLE A HAPPY TUNE

from *The King and I*

Lyrics by Oscar Hammerstein II
Music by Richard Rodgers

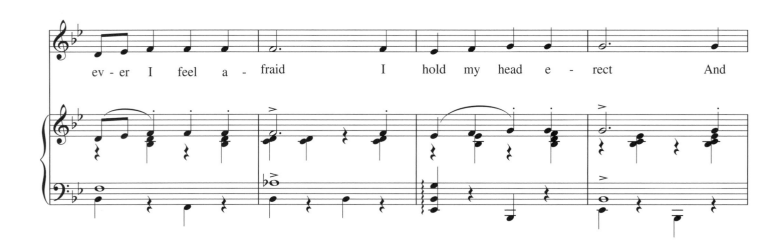

While shiv-er-ing in my shoes I strike a care-less pose And whis-tle a hap-py tune And no one ev-er knows I'm a-fraid _____ The re-sult of this de-cep-tion is ver-y strange to __ tell For when I fool the

peo-ple I fear I fool my-self as well! I whis-tle a hap-py tune And ev-'ry sin-gle time The hap-pi-ness in the tune con-vin-ces me that I'm not a-fraid. Make be-lieve you're brave And the trick will take you far.

You may be as brave as you make be-lieve you are.

Whistle

You may be as brave as you make be-lieve you are.

MY LORD AND MASTER
from *The King and I*

Lyrics by Oscar Hammerstein II
Music by Richard Rodgers

HELLO, YOUNG LOVERS
from *The King and I*

Lyrics by Oscar Hammerstein II
Music by Richard Rodgers

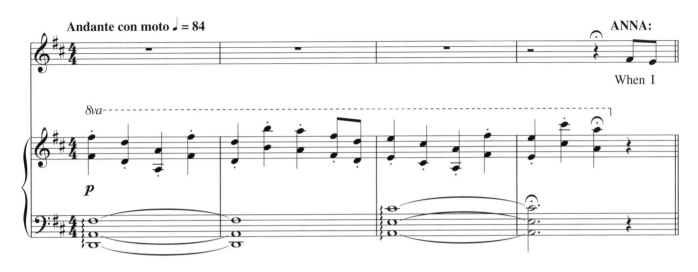

mem - ber this _____ And I al - ways will. _____ There are

new lov - ers now on the same si - lent hill, Look-ing on the same blue sea. And I

know Tom and I are a part of them all, And they're all a part of Tom _____ and

poco rit.

♩. = 50

me. _____ Hel - lo, young lov - ers, Who - ev - er you are, I

mf legato   *p*

hope your trou - bles are few. All my good wish - es go with you to - night

poco rit.

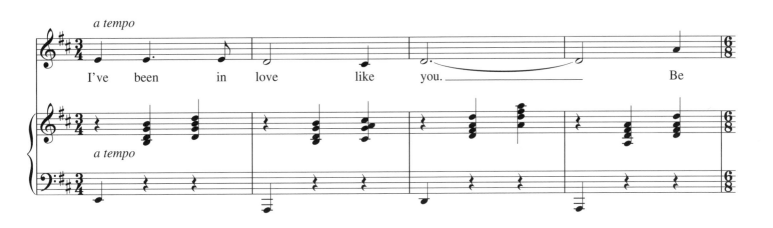

a tempo

I've been in love like you. _____ Be

brave, young lov - ers, and fol - low your star, Be brave and faith - ful and true,

Cling ver - y close to each oth - er to - night. I've been in love like

poco rit. *a tempo*

you. _____ I know how it feels to have wings on your heels, And to fly down a street in a trance. _____ You fly down a street on a chance that you'll meet, And you meet not real - ly by chance. _____ Don't cry, young lov - ers, What-

GETTING TO KNOW YOU

from *The King and I*

Lyrics by Oscar Hammerstein II
Music by Richard Rodgers

learn - ing (You'll for - give me if I boast) And I've now be - come an

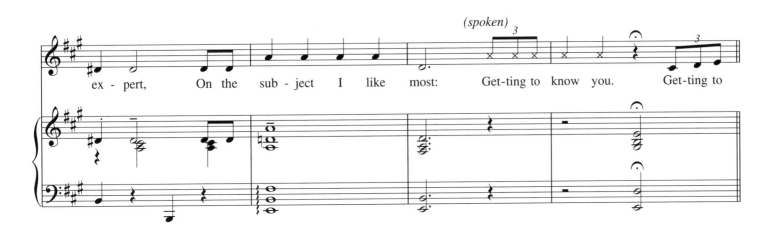

ex - pert, On the sub - ject I like most: *(spoken)* Get-ting to know you. Get-ting to

Gracefully and not fast ♩ = 120

know you, get-ting to know all a - bout you._____ Get-ting to

like you, get-ting to hope you like me _____ Get-ting to

know you, Put-ting it my way, but nice - ly, _____ You are pre-

cresc.

cise - ly _____ My cup of tea! _____ Get-ting to

p

know you, get-ting to feel free and eas - y. _____ When I am

with you, Get-ting to know what to say. _____ Have-n't you

with you. Get-ting to know what to say _____ Have-n't you

no - ticed? Sud-den-ly I'm bright and breez - y _____ Be-cause of

all the beau-ti-ful and new things I'm learn-ing a-bout you

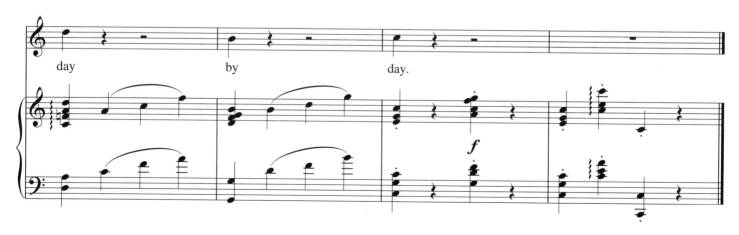

day by day.

WE KISS IN A SHADOW
from *The King and I*

Lyrics by Oscar Hammerstein II
Music by Richard Rodgers

This song is a duet for Lun Tha and Tuptim, adapted as a solo for this edition.

When peo - ple are near, we speak not a word.

A - lone in our se - cret, To - geth - er we sigh For

one smil - ing day to be free,

To kiss in the sun - light And say to the sky:

To kiss in the sun - light

And say to the sky: Be - hold and be -

lieve what you see! Be - hold how my

rit.   *a tempo*   *rit.*

lov - er loves me!

rit.   *pp a tempo*   *rit.*

I HAVE DREAMED
from *The King and I*

Lyrics by Oscar Hammerstein II
Music by Richard Rodgers

so That by now I think I know what it's like to be

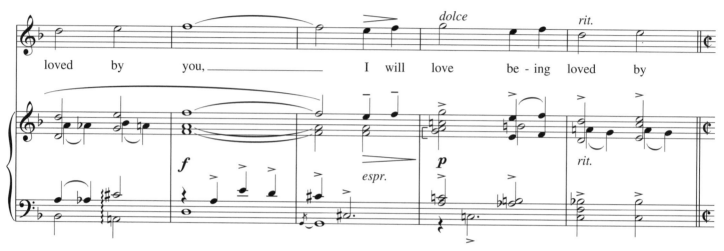

loved by you, _____ I will love be-ing loved by

Poco piu mosso ♩ = 97

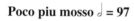

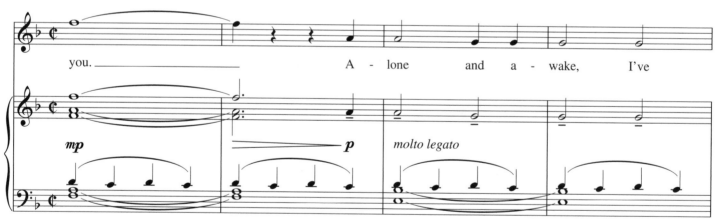

you. _____ A - lone and a - wake, I've

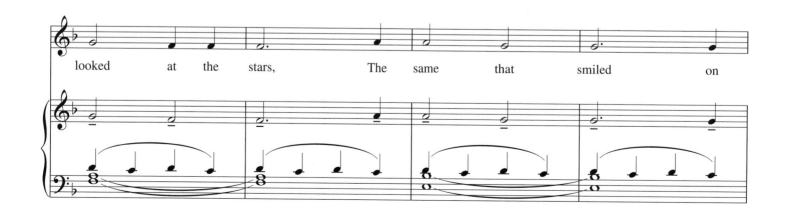

looked at the stars, The same that smiled on

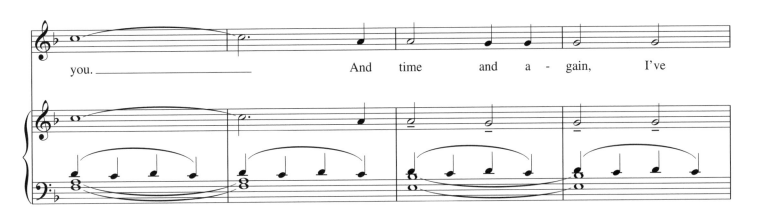

you._____ And time and a-gain, I've

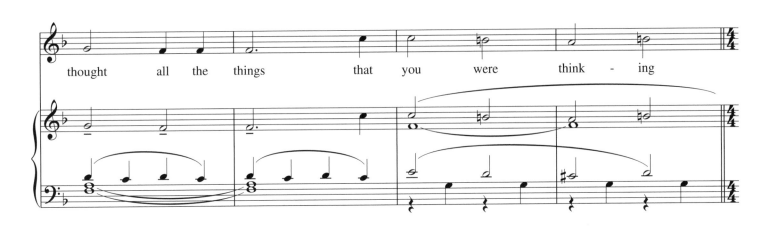

thought all the things that you were think - ing

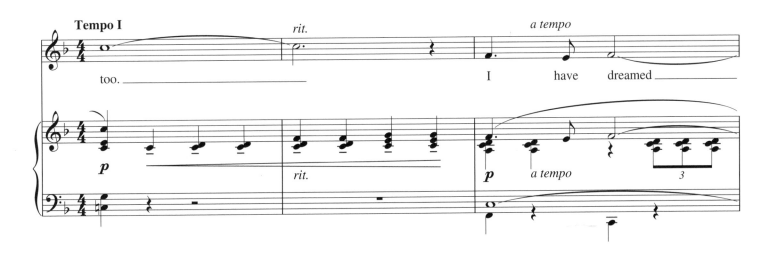

Tempo I *rit.* *a tempo*

too._____ I have dreamed_____

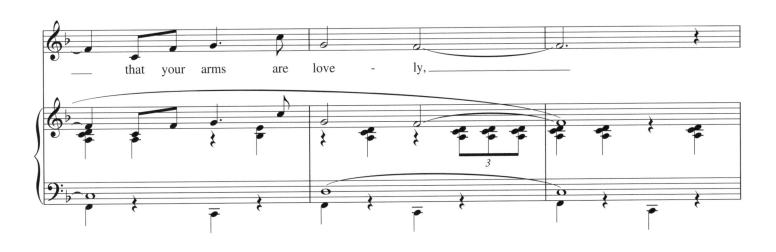

_____ that your arms are love - ly,_____

NO OTHER LOVE
from *Me and Juliet*

Lyrics by Oscar Hammerstein II
Music by Richard Rodgers

Wish-ing that you could be ___ Watch-ing the night with me, ___

In-to the night I cry: Hur-ry home, come

home to me! Set me

free, Free from doubt And

MANY A NEW DAY

from *Oklahoma!*

Lyrics by Oscar Hammerstein II
Music by Richard Rodgers

LAUREY:

Why should a wo-man who is health-y and strong Blub-ber like a ba-by if her man goes a-way? A-weep-in' and a-wail-in' how he's done her wrong, That's one thing you'll nev-er hear me say! Nev-er gon-na think that the

man I lose is the on-ly man a-mong men. I'll snap my fin-gers to

show I don't care, I'll buy me a brand new dress to wear, I'll scrub my neck and I'll

rit.

a tempo

brush my hair And start all o-ver a-gain.

a tempo, con ritmo

Refrain

Con grazia - non legato

Man-y a new face will please my eye, Man-y a new love will find me,

p

Nev-er-'ve I wan-dered through the rye, Won-der-in' where has some

guy gone, Man-y a new day will dawn be-fore I do!

Nev-er-'ve I chased the hon-ey bee who care-less-ly ca-

joled me, Some-bod-y else just as sweet as he, cheered me and con-

OUT OF MY DREAMS

from *Oklahoma!*

Lyrics by Oscar Hammerstein II
Music by Richard Rodgers

IT MIGHT AS WELL BE SPRING

from *State Fair*

Lyrics by Oscar Hammerstein II
Music by Richard Rodgers

star - ry - eyed and vague - ly dis - con - ten - ted, Like a night - in - gale with - out a song to sing. Oh,

why should I have spring fe - ver when it is - n't e - ven spring?

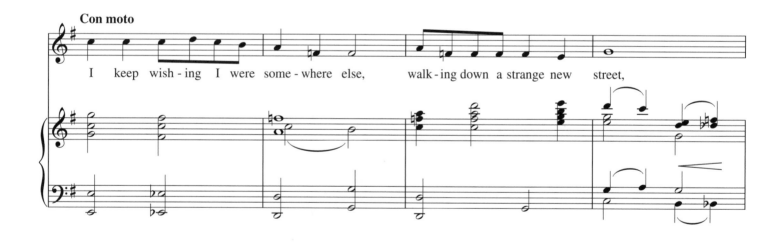

Con moto

I keep wish - ing I were some - where else, walk - ing down a strange new street,

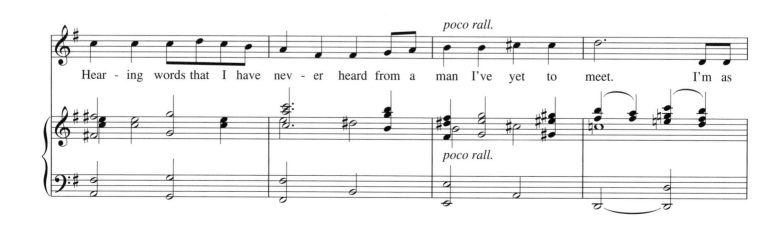

poco rall.

Hear - ing words that I have nev - er heard from a man I've yet to meet. I'm as

poco rall.

MY FAVORITE THINGS
from *The Sound of Music*

Lyrics by Oscar Hammerstein II
Music by Richard Rodgers

Allegro animato

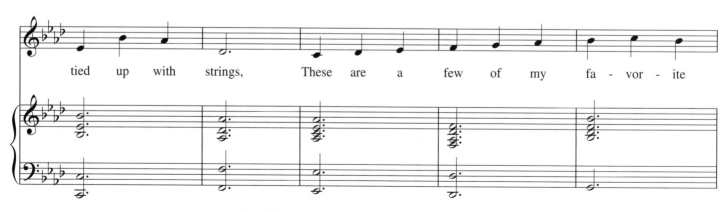

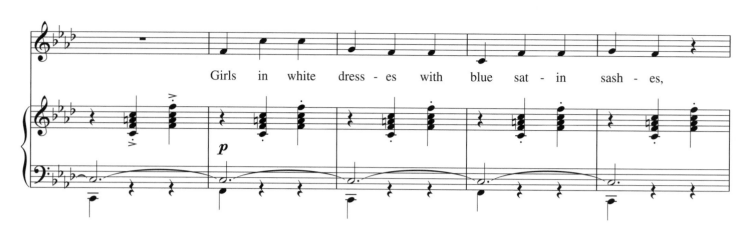

Girls in white dress - es with blue sat - in sash - es,

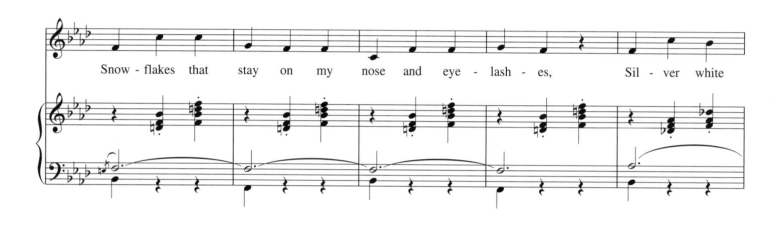

Snow - flakes that stay on my nose and eye - lash - es, Sil - ver white

win - ters that melt in - to springs, These are a few of my

fa - vor - ite things. When the dog bites, When the

poco marcato

dress - es with blue sat - in sash - es, Snow - flakes that stay on my

nose and eye - lash - es, Sil - ver white win - ters that melt in - to

springs, These are a few of my fa - vor - ite things.

When the dog bites, When the bee stings,

When I'm feel - ing sad, _____ I sim - ply re - mem - ber my fa - vor - ite things and then I don't feel _____ so bad. _____

CLIMB EV'RY MOUNTAIN
from *The Sound of Music*

Lyrics by Oscar Hammerstein II
Music by Richard Rodgers

THE SOUND OF MUSIC
from *The Sound of Music*

Lyrics by Oscar Hammerstein II
Music by Richard Rodgers

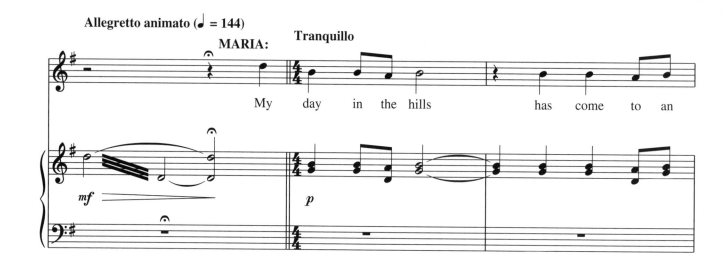

My day in the hills has come to an

end, I know. A star has come out to tell me it's

time to go. But deep in the dark green shad-ows are

years. _____ The hills fill my heart with the sound of

mu - sic. _____ My heart wants to sing ev - 'ry song it

hears. _____ My heart wants to beat like the wings of the birds that rise from the

lake to the trees. My heart wants to sigh like a chime that flies from a

The optional high note is an editorial suggestion for consideration.